Turn backward

Walter Kubilius

Alpha Editions

This edition published in 2024

ISBN : 9789362512055

Design and Setting By
Alpha Editions
www.alphaedis.com
Email - info@alphaedis.com

Contents

TURN BACKWARD, O TIME!

BY WALTER KUBILIUS

The one hope for Donovan was to
escape into the past, become a
citizen of the early 20th Century.
But he overlooked the aftermath....

"Adel W. Crane, C.D." Donovan held the Identi-plast in his hands, the fingers trembling slightly. "What do the letters 'C.D.' stand for?" he asked, determined to play the part of an honest citizen who had no interest in unlicensed rejuvenation or time travel.

The chalk-faced young man with the fixed smile told him: "Cyclic Detection. You may have heard our more dramatic nickname, Criminal Destroyers; I've been an agent since 2452."

High-strung Donovan moistened his lips. Of course he had heard of the C.D. In an age when cyclic travel backward through the centuries was an established science, the Komitet that governed the Home Planet had to employ ruthless measures to cope with any experimenters whose uncontrolled work might threaten to change past temporal cycles. The C.D. were the scavengers of the World Komitet; they scoured the past centuries eliminating illegal and unlicensed cyclic travellers. In a rigidly-controlled solar system there were thousands of law-breakers, political disappointees, and even youth-seekers like Donovan, who hoped for life-extensions in past ages. The C.D., with terror and all the resources of the solar system, hunted them down and exterminated them. Quietly, ruthlessly, and painfully.

"The criminal Blascomb," Crane said, the fixed smile still on the thin lips, "has been observed near the Donovan metallurgical plants. The Komitet suspects that someone close to your office may have established contact with him for illegal rejuvenation."

His eyes left Donovan's taut face and scanned the office walls. Control boards recording operations in extra-terrestial metallin plants lined two sides of the office. The only break in the sternness of the walls was an antique painting, a still-life abstraction that must have dated way back to the 20th century. Crane stared at its flashes of color, the fixed smile turning to amused contempt.

Donovan dared not ask for additional details. The word or whim of the Komitet was law. Criminal Destroyer! Donovan shuddered; he had spent the past six months in quietly transferring ownership of the Trust to various fronts for Blascomb. A fortune worth several erg-units squared to the 6th power had already changed hands. Had the C.D. caught him before Blascomb could deliver on the rejuvenation and time-escape deal?

"We have nothing to hide," Donovan said, "my staff will cooperate with the C.D. I assume you want access to the psycho-record files?"

Edel W. Crane, contemptuous eyes turning away from the still-life, reached a bony hand for the approval slip.

"I will let you know what I find."

Donovan stood up, and when the C.D. agent left he frantically sent out a conscious call to Blascomb's thought-frequency number.

"By the Komitet!" Blascomb's wave-induced voice rang in Donovan's ears, "I told you never to call me unless it was most urgent."

"This is urgent," Donovan thought desperately, "Crane, a C.D. agent, was here a minute ago. He's going to look over the books of the Trust."

"He won't find a thing," Blascomb's thoughts were confident in Donovan's mind, "They haven't caught a single one of the men I've sent back into the 17th century; just be patient and we'll cyclic you out within a week."

"Then hurry. My heart's in bad shape and I can't last much longer. I'm practically being kept alive by that rotten Callistan serum."

"Stay alive for one more week," Blascomb thought encouragingly, "and you'll be young for centuries."

Turn backward, turn backward, O Time in thy flight! The song sped through Donovan's mind, lifting his spirits. To be young again, and to be free from the constant supervision and threat of the terrifying C.D.!

"As for Crane," Blascomb went on, "It's part of the service I'm giving you. We've arranged a false-lead case in your office. Crane has his talons set for your brother-in-law. Shortly before the C.D. annihilates him your escape will be arranged to throw suspicion upon him. We will make it seem that your brother-in-law killed you for denouncing him to the C.D. Crane will never see through the subterfuge; you'll be safe—perhaps forever."

His brother-in-law's life was a cheap price to pay for youth. Donovan stared at his stiff, corpse-like hands. All he needed was one more week. He would make one more effort to secure a Life-Extension—and then....

The Examiner for the Board of Life waited while Donovan dressed. The answer could already be seen in the official's eyes.

"No?"

"I'm sorry," the Examiner said, "but the laws of the Komitet are fairly stringent. Only those whose social value is above Par 195 may be rejuvenated. Not much value is placed upon engineers and Trust managers who can easily be replaced from each year's Birth Quota. The application is denied, and there's no use appealing it."

"It's unjust!" Donovan exclaimed, ignoring the alarming pain in his failing heart. "All I want is ten more years—not even a full return to youth! If there's no room on Home Planet, let me go the extra-terrestials or even some asteroid. I'll make any contribution required to...."

The Examiner, who had often heard such vain pleas, rapped his desk with the blood-analyscope. "The Komitet is far too wise to permit socially unnecessary extensions of the life span, just as it does not permit unlicensed time travel. What would happen if we allowed you to be rejuvenated, and then permitted extra-terrestial emigration? There would be millions of old or sick people like you demanding equal treatment and equal consideration. Before long the planets and asteroids would be overpopulated and independent colonies set up thereon which would eventually come in conflict with the Home Planet Komitet. No, my friend, the Komitet is wise in decreeing that rejuvenation and human birth are mutually contradictory. Rather than sacrifice birth, with the consequent stagnation of the human species, the Komitet has decided rigidly to control youth-extensions, and grants those periods of additional life only to the socially valuable."

"Yes," Donovan said bitterly, "the Komitet keeps itself immortal while the rest of us have to die."

The Examiner's voice was hard. "Shall I denounce you to the C.D.?"

"I beg forgiveness," Donovan said; "your decision is a just one and I shall make no appeal."

Blascomb had a very persistent thought-call. Donovan relaxed in the office chair and let his consciousness-levels sink to the call-number.

"This is the moment," the thought patterns registered. "The C.D. is about to close in with the faked evidence we've prepared. Your brother-in-law's about to call. Trust in me; all is ready. Do not become frightened, for excessive adrenalin might upset the required endocrine balance."

Before he could frame a reply, Blascomb's thought faded away. The office door slid open and Edel W. Crane walked in. Donovan's heart throbbed painfully: was this an unexpected crisis in their plans, or had Blascomb prepared even this?

"The C.D.'s finished its analysis," Crane said, "I thought you might be interested."

"Naturally, I—"

"The case was very simple. I wish citizens would realize that they cannot fight against the enormous resources of the C.D. We will destroy—"

The public-screen flashed urgently. Donovan excused himself and turned the knob. His brother-in-law's angry face switched into view.

"Donovan! That was a dirty rotten thing to do. What right did you have to denounce me to the C.D.? I should kill you for this!"

Donovan's bewilderment was genuine. He felt Crane's eyes upon him, and a thrill of admiration for Blascomb's genius suddenly swept through him.

"What do you want?" he managed to say.

"I've got to see you immediately. I'm downstairs, in back of the pilo-cab station."

"Later—"

"Now!"

The image snapped off. Donovan turned to the C.D. agent. "'Scuse me for a moment," he stammered, "some family trouble. I'll be back in a short while."

Crane glanced up. "I'll wait."

Donovan walked through his office, conscious that he was doing this for the last time. Rejuvenation was like death. You put an end to a lifetime casually and without haste.

At the pilo-cab station, the wind cutting down from the whirr of swooping cabs, Donovan met Blascomb. There were two bright flashes, and then the smell of disintegrated flesh. Blascomb gestured toward two graying pools on the plasticized floor in back of them.

"Murder and suicide," he said, obviously pleased with himself, "The C.D. will think you are dead. The murderer's body is also there to provide a motive for the transfer of the Trust's funds in the event Crane becomes too thorough. He'll be here soon; we work fast now."

The special pilo-cab dropped them into a gravity-shielded warehouse above the European Desert. It housed Blascomb's laboratory. The rejuvenation process was even simpler than Donovan had expected.

"Not the Fountain of Youth, exactly," Blascomb explained as he plunged in the needle, "but a selective antibody that attacks only aging tissue and forces replacements practically on an embryonic level of activity. Unlike the Callistan serum, which is merely a stimulant, this antibody creates from its destroyed tissue a catalyst capable of stimulating chromosomes and genes. By the very process of feeding upon itself, the body grows younger. The net result is a reversal of the life process, an anabolism making you grow younger, year by year."

"Eventually to disappear as a single cell?"

"Ultimately, yes. Long before that period, probably when you're a young man, you'll have to return to 2482 for a reversion to normal metabolism."

"The process can be repeated?"

"Indefinitely."

Donovan breathed deeply. "Immortality!"

Blascomb did not smile. "Only if the C.D. does not find you. Unlicensed rejuvenation is punishable by execution in an extremely painful manner. You're a doomed man now if the C.D. even finds you. The worst tortures of the Middle Ages would be nothing compared to what Crane would do to you or me if he tracks us down."

"You can stay in the present time-cycle," Donovan said, "but I'm tired of control and supervision. Send me to some period where an individual had a chance to work and live without state control. Give me the times of individualism!"

"C.D. agents are everywhere in the time-cycles, tracking down illegal immigrants. Quite a number of the men I've rejuvenated chose the Renaissance for escape, but I'm afraid that a good part of that cycle's carnage was the work of such C.D. agents as our friend Crane. I'd recommend another period."

"The Golden Age of Greece?"

Blascomb shook his head. "Already taken. Aristotle, Plato, and a few others are 25th century men. Archimedes was murdered by a C.D. agent, and Socrates sent to his death by a group of them."

"Their fates were known to history—why did those men leave the 25th century to live in that cycle?"

He shrugged his shoulders. "They probably felt that the few years of extra life were worth it. Well, into what period do you want to go and what would you do there?"

"I do not understand the paradoxes," Donovan said, "What if I chose to build gravity-deflectors in Ancient Rome?"

"It would be impossible because there were no such manufacturers then. It would mean that you were either promptly killed by a C.D. agent who recognized the anachronistic attempt, or you had changed your mind."

"But if I can choose any period, it means that I can alter history at will—which presumes that the present can also be changed."

"That is what the Komitet believes, and that is why the C.D. is so ruthless and brutal with unlicensed time travellers. The real answer is that in the final analysis your decision to choose a certain time period is already made, and the things you will do are already determined. Free will is an illusion; it is synonymous with incomplete perception."

"Then send me into the 20th century. As an engineer I would be able to make some sort of living there."

"Dangerous. Don't practice your profession. Study some field which is completely alien to you so that should you come across a C.D. agent he would not recognize the work of a 25th century man."

"You mean like an artist or a writer?"

"Why not?"

Donovan laughed. "I've never held a paint brush or written more than a one-page letter, but why not? Unloose the cyclic band, Blascomb; set me loose in the 20th century, and give my regards to the C.D.!"

In the dimly lighted garret above the tavern, Donovan stood before his easel. His face was no longer lined, for the past twenty-five years had made him a much younger man. He had taken Blascomb's advice and had studied a field completely alien to him. In his own time, the 25th century, his paintings would have been considered laughably amateurish, but for 1926 they were infinitely superior to anything produced by 20th century artists.

"Why can't they *see*?" he asked his agent angrily, when his third show passed without the sale of a single painting.

"I can see them," the agent said, standing in front of a still-life abstraction with flashes of color, "but your way of working is too far advanced for our time. Believe me, a few hundred years from now your paintings will be regarded as the work of a great genius."

"In the meantime, I starve."

"I can help you."

Donovan threw down the paint brushes. "No. No. There's no use being ahead of one's time. I can't make a living as an artist. I may as well go back to digging ditches."

"Maybe you can work part-time and paint at night. What did you do before you started painting?"

He hesitated, but what was there to be afraid of? "I—I was an engineer."

"I can get you a job with a construction company."

"No. No! I want nothing whatever to do with engineering! Nothing!"

In the 25 years that he had lived in the 20th century he had turned from a man of 65 to a healthy, robust 40. For a long time he had lived in fear that the dreaded arms of the C.D. would reach out for him, and that he would stand face to face with terror-inspiring Crane. But he had never met anyone who seemed to be a C.D., a Criminal Destroyer. Sometimes he felt the avenging sword of the Komitet hanging over his head.

There were some statesmen and philosophers mentioned in the newspapers whose ideas seemed to indicate a 25th century origin, but he avoided them in the fear that they might be plants to draw out the illegals. It was probably that the C.D. would never find out the deception, and if they did there was little chance of locating him among the two billion people on Home Planet.

"You have to make a living somehow," the agent persisted.

"I know nothing but engineering," Donovan said, "and that I will never do."

"Maybe there's some other field in which you could use engineering skills." He thought for a moment, and then reached into his briefcase. "I picked this up on a newsstand. You might like it."

Donovan glanced at the magazine's cover.

"It's the latest thrill—scientific fiction. Maybe with your engineering knowledge you could write a story or two."

When the agent left, Donovan read through the magazine, then went out to look up other stories of the same nature. One story offered a time-travel theory which was absurdly inaccurate. Another purported to deal with the inhabitants of Mars, none of which looked at all the way the writers imagined them to be. Donovan read as many as he could find, and was fascinated by the hopeless incompetence and scientific inaccuracy of the so-called writers. The time-travel story was laughable; even a child could produce a far more exciting tale by describing the Watson-Gorshevich experiments that lead to the discovery of repetitive time-cycles back in 2364.

Why not, he thought to himself. *Why not write these stories of the future? Who could do them better than a man who had come from the future?* These were not engineering journals where accuracy was required, nor would anyone ever act upon the scientific discoveries he might record. Above all, no one would attempt to build any machines which would immediately attract the attention of the C.D. He would do nothing which would in the slightest way affect historic development.

Pressed by the need for money, and fascinated by the possibilities in science fiction, Donovan began to write a story. He employed a pen-name, and avoided the general theory of retrograde-cycle travel backward above time, but limited himself to travelling spirally into the future. He described the mechanism he himself would have to produce in order to get back to Blascomb for anabolism-correction, and produced a fanciful tale regarding life in the year 3,000. The letter from the editor came within a week.

Dear Mr. Donovan:

Enclosed find check for your story, "Turn Backward, O Time!" I have seldom read a more convincing fantasy. One could almost believe that the apparatus you described would actually work. I believe this story will be a science-fiction classic and am placing your original manuscript in my collection. I would appreciate seeing other examples of your work.

When the story appeared in print, several paragraphs describing the construction of the time-machine were omitted by the editor. "Technically unconvincing," they told him; "they mar up the verisimilitude of a great story." "Turn Backward, O Time!" became an instant success.

A few days later, Donovan contributed another story, this time based on actual events on Jupiter which he simply transferred to a different time-cycle on Vega. Vaguely recalling some warning of Blascomb's that while the future could not be changed, it was best to play safe and not draw the attention of the C.D., he twisted and changed all the scientific facts involved. The check for the second story was promptly sent.

Within a few months Donovan, under his pseudonym, which was kept secret, was launched upon his career as a writer of science fiction. Readers praised him for his convincing fantasy and editors competed for his services.

Memory of the 25th century gradually faded from his mind as years passed. At times he awoke in horror after nightmares that Crane of the C.D. had finally caught him, but these terrifying dreams became rarer. He had exposed himself repeatedly in fiction. Time and time again he had described actual historical events of the Space Colony Wars in his stories. On one occasion he described the technique for the cure of cancer discovered in 2019. The readers' section of the magazine soon carried letters from doctors who were amused that a writer could present such a simple household remedy and dare suggest that it might be efficacious for cancer.

Donovan was amused by the thought that Crane might be diligently searching for him somewhere in the Renaissance; if so, the C.D. agent's fury must be mounting.

He changed his name and identity every ten years to conceal his gradual return to youth. He had the pleasure of seeing himself hailed as his successor in popularity, as he established new names and let the older ones die out. His excuse to the editors was that he wanted to enter into competition anew, make sure that his name alone was not carrying the stories. He was happy. Sometimes, however, later stories were panned by "fans" as "imitations of the classics by the greatest stf writer the world has ever known."

Only the aging gentleman who had bought Donovan's first manuscript knew, but the old man signed the checks and said nothing.

In his happiness and self-satisfaction, Donovan became more careless with his stories. If he had been able to outwit Crane and the dreaded C.D., surely he could dash off stories good enough for the poor minds of 20th century science-fiction readers!

Then the tide turned. Fan letters in the magazines began really to tear into his fiction; they *were* third-rate; they lacked imagination. They were ordinary stories written by an ordinary mind; and science fiction required tales written by men whose minds were well ahead of 20th century thought. The day finally came when all the editors began rejecting his stories. First one, then another—and finally every story written received a rejection slip.

Donovan could not understand the reason for the change. A few years ago—or was it decades?—each story of his was labelled a "classic"; now they were not even acceptable. Had science fiction changed so much since his decision to become a writer in 1929? He dared not discuss it with anyone, for he had no friends and he trusted no one. The C.D. was everywhere, but there was one man in whom he had the deepest confidence.

Donovan visited the aging editor and felt sorry for the worn-out old man. He himself had once been like this, but was now free from death. He thought of taking his benefactor with him into the 25th century and saving the editor's life. But suppose Blascomb's laboratory had been captured? Donovan could manage for himself, but it would be cruel to leave the old man in the deadly hands of the C.D. No, it was best to say nothing about rejuvenation to the editor; he would only think Donovan was trying out a story-idea.

"I've been your editor for thirty years," the old man's voice cracked. His half-blind eyes loomed through thick lenses.

"It's been a long time," Donovan said.

"My—My eyes are not what they used to be," the other said, "A man about 50 years old wrote that great classic, "Turn Backward, O Time!" He must be about 80 now. But you look only 20. Ah, laddie, you're trying to fool me. You must be his son!"

"That's right," Donovan said quickly, "We have the same name."

"Then that explains it," the other said wearily; "it would break my old heart if a talent like your father's disintegrated. But we came to talk about your stories. No, son, you're not the writer your father was. Your tales lack imagination; there is no originality in them. The ideas are hackneyed, the writing third-rate. They sound like poor imitations of the great tales told by your father. There was a man! There was a writer!"

Donovan left him, keeping the secret of his identity. When he returned to his home he looked in the mirror, and the face of a rose-cheeked 20-year-old youngster stared back at him. Fifty years of happy living in the 20th century! It would soon be necessary to return to the 25th century so that Blascomb could reverse the antibiotic catalytic process that had set him growing younger. It was impossible to stay in his present youthful state much longer. In a few years he would be a child.

With a sigh he walked to his desk, took out paper and pen, and began to draw the diagrams for the apparatus which would send him forward into the 25th century.

For three hours he worked confidently, and then the sweat began to drip from his forehead and his heart began to pound fearfully. "It is not possible," he said, uneasily. "It will all come back to me soon. Now what the devil did Blascomb tell me?"

He had become lazy, and his brain was not used to hard work. He said this to himself but he could not shake off the sense of fear. He took a cold shower, rubbing himself briskly, then shot a stimulant into his blood stream. Preparing the desk once more, he began to work.

The papers gathered, the pencils broke, and the night gradually turned to morning. The finished sketch of the cycle travellers was basically correct, but the most important operating mechanism was still missing. Try as he could, he was unable to bring it up from his memory.

"By the solar system," he swore, "what is the matter with me? I have forgotten every detail."

He tried to think back. At one time he had known the mechanism thoroughly. As an engineer he was completely familiar with every single plate and tube, but now he couldn't remember anything but the general appearance of the finished machine. Fear spurred his mind as he hunted for a solution. Something was happening to his mind. He began to think of his stories. The same thing had happened there. At one time he remembered every detail of life in the 25th century, and could describe them easily. Now events were dim and he knew now why his recent stories were poor. They were not written from actual memory of the future, but were the ordinary stories one might expect from a 20-year-old boy. The past was dim and memory faded. Blascomb and Crane, Crane and Blascomb, which was the C.D. agent, and what was C.D. anyway?

Enough of the details remained to shock him into an awareness of his desperate plight. The rejuvenation process had worked too well, for Donovan had waited dangerously long. As the body grew younger the tissue cells were consumed and youthful cells replaced them. The process that had worked for body cells did the same for the cells of the brain. Those portions of the brain containing the knowledge and ability of a 70-year-old man were gradually being replaced with new, untrained cells. He had failed to re-educate himself as new cells replaced the old, and had come to the brink of disaster.

Sufficient intelligence and manual dexterity remained to compensate for that, but in a few years the task would be hopeless.

Excitedly, for he knew his life depended on it, he rummaged through his book shelves looking for a copy of his first story, "Turn Backward, O Time!" It contained, he remembered, a concise, accurate description of the mechanism for the time-machine. The magazine itself was old, the sheets turning brown and the pages breaking. He read the story in haste, vaguely remembering the plot. The actual description of the operating mechanism, he found to his consternation, was missing. "I will cut one or two paragraphs," the editor had said, *"They are not convincing, technically ... they lack verisimilitude!"*

Not convincing! If he did not find them he was doomed to become a child, and then a babbling idiot of a baby and would disappear entirely within twenty years. He telephoned the magazine's office and asked for the editor.

"Sorrree," the secretary said, "Mr. O'Sloane is quite ill. The doctors are afraid he might not pass through the night. He's very old, you know."

"Can he speak?" Donovan asked desperately.

"He's had a stroke. Can't say a word. Completely paralyzed, Sorrreee."

Donovan cursed the carelessness that had led him to this difficult position. He knew that O'Sloane kept the originals of his favorite stories in a collection in his office. If O'Sloane died it was possible that some enterprising youthful editor would destroy the old manuscripts in a fit of house-cleaning.

"This is Donovan," he said quickly, "I am trying to locate the original copy of "Turn Backward, O Time" which O'Sloane has in his files. I must study the original papers; it's extremely important. If there is a substitute editor, will you ask him to keep an eye open for it."

"Cerrrtainleee."

He sighed and took a taxi to the editorial office. It would be best to get it as quickly as possible. The original manuscript was quite safe. Donovan need only copy the original description. Even if he were no longer able to grasp the theory of it, the machine was still easy enough to build from the description.

Within a few hours he would be back in the 25th century for a reversal. For his next trip back he would choose Ancient Egypt. The 20th century was heading for the Atomic Wars and he was fortunate in being able to escape. After Egypt he would choose the Inca civilization. Did they not have legends of white gods that ruled them? The world was his, and he would be forever young. Immortality was within his grasp. No one could stop him now.

He arrived at the building and rushed up the steps to the editorial office.

"We found the manuscript, Mr. Donovan," the secretary told him brightly, looking twice at the flushed, handsome face.

Donovan stepped into O'Sloane's office. Practically nothing had been touched as yet, for one of the staff editors had just begun to sort a pile of stacked papers from several cabinets. Donovan recognized the original manuscript of "Turn Backward, O Time!" upon the desk, and hurriedly skimmed through the pages. The description was intact, and while he could not remember why such a machine would work, he knew that it could be built and he could escape.

With a sigh he pocketed the manuscript and introduced himself to the young editor who would probably succeed O'Sloane upon his death.

"Oh yes," the editor with the curious thin smile said, "I have heard quite a bit about you, and have been waiting a long time for this meeting. We've met before, you know."

"Really?" Donovan said. The face did appear familiar, but he could not recall the occasion.

"My name is Edel W. Crane, C.D."

Donovan felt a cold tremor of fear shake his body.

He moistened his lips.

"What do the letters C.D. stand for?"

The pasty-faced young man closed and then locked the door of the office. Walking towards Donovan, the smile no longer there, he told him. Then he did what he had come to do.

Milton Keynes UK
Ingram Content Group UK Ltd.
UKHW030839021124
450589UK00006B/669

9 789362 512055